PAPER SUPERPLANES

Peter Holland and Kate Needham

Designed by Ian McNee

Illustrated by Angie Sage

Contents

2 Getting started

4 Square-o-plane
6 Delta wing
8 Flying squirrel
10 Tiny trainers
(V jet, A10 Warthog)

12 Camber jet

14 Stunt bug
16 Seagull

18 Concorde
20 Sky rocket
22 Swing wing
24 Superglider
29 Templates

First published in 1992 Usborne Publishing Ltd,
Usborne House, 83-85 Saffron Hill, London EC1N 8RT,
England. Copyright © 1992 Usborne Publishing Ltd.

The name Usborne and the device ☜ are Trade
Marks of Usborne Publishing Ltd. All rights reserved. UE

Getting started

This book shows you how to make lots of amazing paper planes and tells you how to fly them. It starts with small models, marked ☆, that you make up quickly from a single piece of paper. The ones marked ☆☆☆ are much bigger and take a couple of hours to put together carefully. These two pages tell you all the things you need to know before you start.

What sort of paper?

It is very important to have the right type of paper for each model. If it is too floppy or too heavy the plane will not fly well. This book talks about the three different thicknesses of paper shown below:

How to score a line

Scoring a line is when you make a firm crease in the paper. Score lines are used to fold along, or to strengthen a wing. You make one like this:

Put a ruler along the line you want to score. Hold it there firmly.

Use a ball point pen to draw a line against the ruler. Press hard to make a firm crease.

Things you will need

Thin cardboard such as the sort used for cereal packets.

Strong white glue, such as PVA or UHU.

Plasticine*

Stick of glue

Scissors

Pencil

Stiff paper, about the thickness of the pages in this book, such as top quality writing paper or envelopes.

Normal paper, such as ordinary writing paper or photocopy paper.

An old ball-point pen to score with — if it has run out of ink it won't mark your plane.

Ruler

Sticky tape-masking tape is best because it peels off easily.

Metal paper-clips

Tracing paper

*U.S. Plastic modelling compound.

Folding

When you make a paper plane it is very important to fold accurately and neatly.

Press down in the middle first. Then smooth out to the sides.

For long folds, place the line you want to fold along on the edge of a table. Then press down against it.

Decoration

Only use decorations that won't change the shape or weight of your plane. You could start with coloured paper or use felt tip pens to draw on patterns afterwards.

Wet paints make the paper wrinkle. Enamel paints are too heavy.

Spray paints shrink the paper and make it curl.

Launching a plane

These angles must be the same.

Before you launch a plane, always check to see that both sides look exactly the same and that the wings tilt up at the same angle on each side.

Light models with big wings, like squirrel and superglider, fly slowly so you need to launch them gently. Move your whole arm slowly forwards and then let go.

Heavier models with smaller wings, like stunt bug and sky rocket, fly faster and need harder launches. Throw them very slightly upwards.

3

Square-o-plane

This simple design shows you what makes a paper plane fly. Use a normal piece of paper, such as ordinary writing paper, 21 x 15cm (6 x 8in).

Make the last score line here.

Middle

7.5cm (3in) 7.5cm (3in)

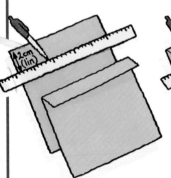

Use felt tip pens to draw on a face or bright pattern.

1. Score a line 2cm (1in) from the top of one short edge (see 'How to score' on page 2). Then fold along it.

2. Score another line at the edge of the last fold and fold over again. Then repeat this once more.

3. Turn the paper over so that the folded edge is underneath. Mark the middle of each short edge.

Long edges

2cm (1in)

2cm (1in)

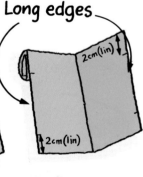

short edges

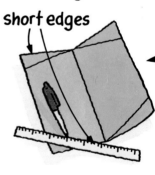

Use a large metal paper-clip. Put it in the middle.

Bend down

Bend up

4. Score a line down the centre. Fold along it, then unfold it, so that the sides tilt up slightly.

5. Make a pencil dot on the long edges, 2cm (1in) from each corner as shown.

6. Score a line from each pencil dot to the centre of the short edge.

7. Bend the front corners down slightly and the back corners up. Add a paper-clip to the front edge.

4

Before you launch your plane, check that it looks like the pictures below from the side and the front.

Side view

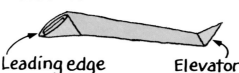

Leading edge   **Elevator**

The front edge needs to be heavier. It is called the leading edge. The back corners tilt up and are called elevators. They help stop the plane from rocking.

Front view

The wings tilt slightly up at exactly the same angle. This is called dihedral. It makes the plane glide steadily.

To launch the square-o-plane

Hold the plane at the back with one finger on top. Launch with a gentle push. Don't throw it, just let go. If it doesn't make a perfect glide, try changing the balance as described below.

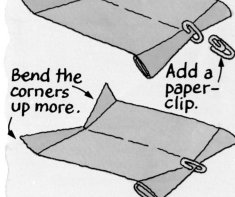

Bend the corners up more.

Add a paper-clip.

A stall is when the tail drops down because the nose is not heavy enough. Add another paper-clip or flatten out the elevators.

A dive is when the nose drops down because it is too heavy. Bend the back corners up, or take away a paper-clip.

Perfect glide

Stall

A slight stall may mean you launched it too fast.

Dive

A slight dive may mean you launched it too slowly.

5

Delta wing

You need a piece of normal paper 20cm x 28cm (8in x 11in). Have the short edges of the paper at the sides.

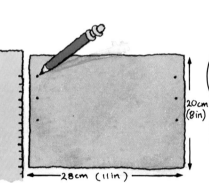

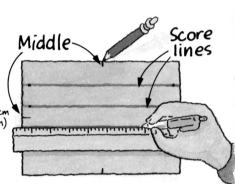

Tip

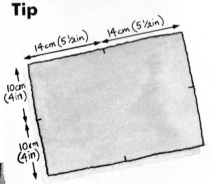

1. Make a pencil dot 4cm, 8cm and 12cm (1½in, 3in and 4½in) below the top edge, on both sides.

2. Score a line between each pair of dots. Then mark the middle of each edge.

To find the middle of the side edges, measure 10cm (4in) from each corner. For the long edges measure 14cm (5½in).

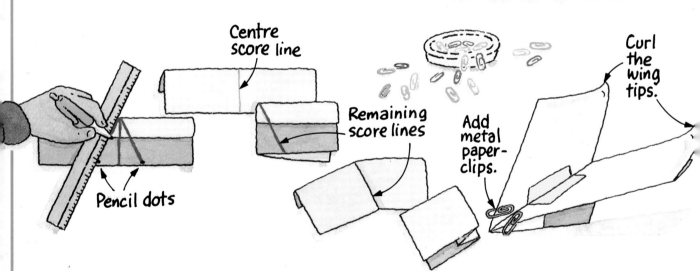

7. Score a line from each dot to the centre of the folded edge.

8. Turn the paper over. Then fold it down the centre score line.

9. Fold the wings back along the remaining score lines.

10. Make the wings stick out to the side. Tape down the middle and add paper-clips.

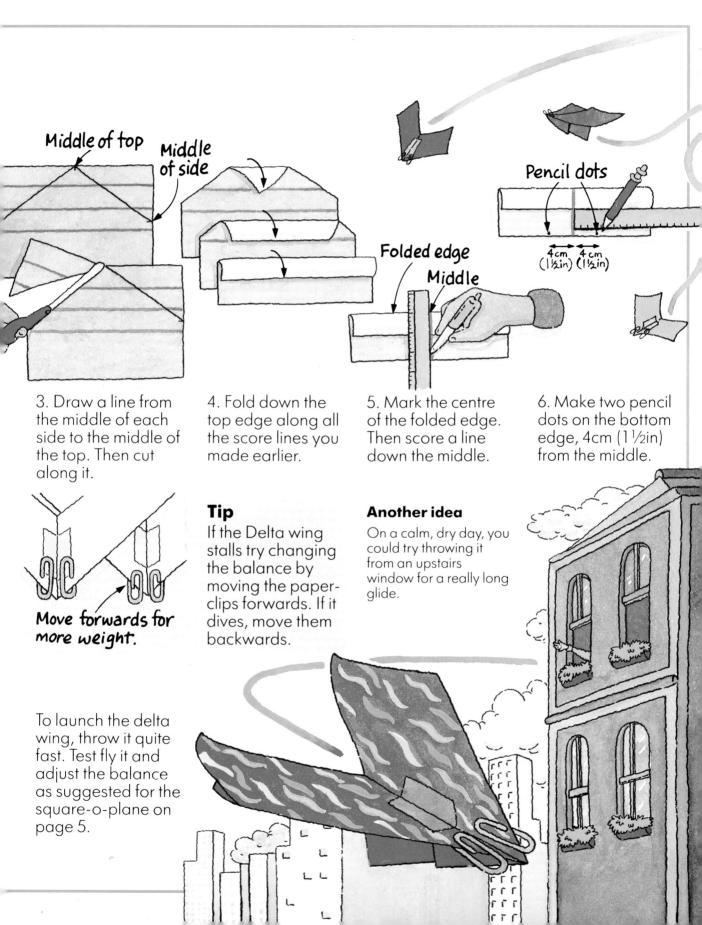

Middle of top
Middle of side

Pencil dots

4cm (1½in) 4cm (1½in)

Folded edge
Middle

3. Draw a line from the middle of each side to the middle of the top. Then cut along it.

4. Fold down the top edge along all the score lines you made earlier.

5. Mark the centre of the folded edge. Then score a line down the middle.

6. Make two pencil dots on the bottom edge, 4cm (1½in) from the middle.

Move forwards for more weight.

Tip
If the Delta wing stalls try changing the balance by moving the paper-clips forwards. If it dives, move them backwards.

Another idea
On a calm, dry day, you could try throwing it from an upstairs window for a really long glide.

To launch the delta wing, throw it quite fast. Test fly it and adjust the balance as suggested for the square-o-plane on page 5.

Flying squirrel

Lots of models in this book use templates. It tells you how to copy a template on page 29. For the squirrel you need the green one on page 30.

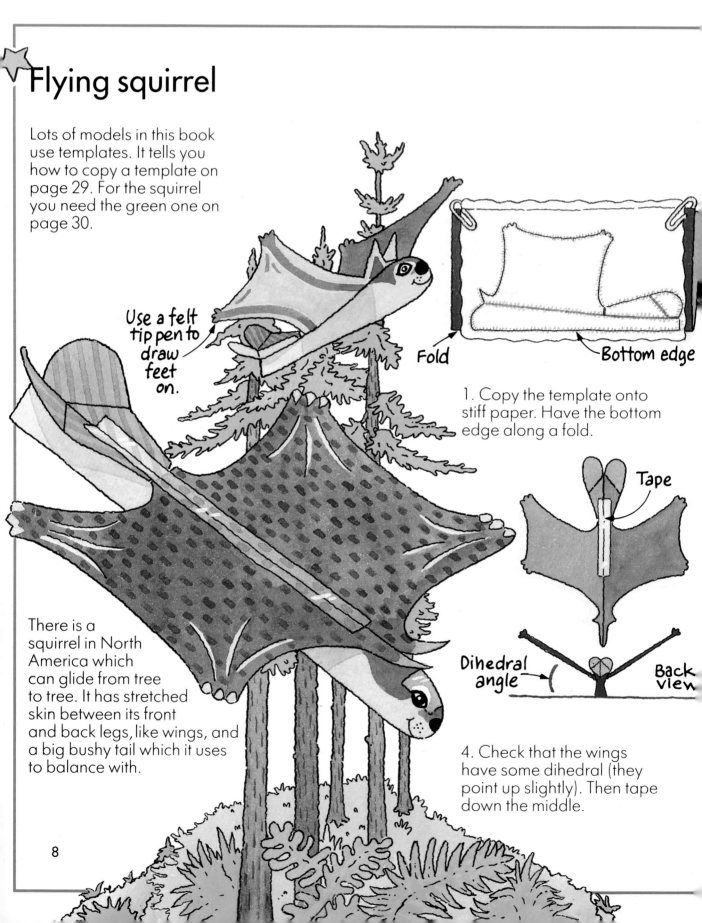

Use a felt tip pen to draw feet on.

Fold

Bottom edge

1. Copy the template onto stiff paper. Have the bottom edge along a fold.

Tape

There is a squirrel in North America which can glide from tree to tree. It has stretched skin between its front and back legs, like wings, and a big bushy tail which it uses to balance with.

Dihedral angle

Back view

4. Check that the wings have some dihedral (they point up slightly). Then tape down the middle.

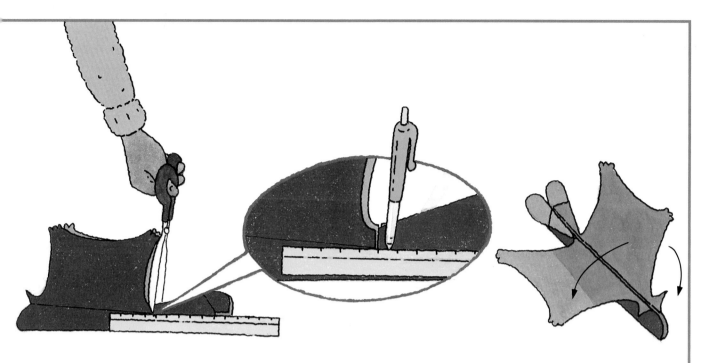

2. Cut along the red lines and score the blue ones. The blue line changes angle at the slit, so you will need to score each side separately.

3. Bend the wings and tail out to the side along the score lines.

Tip

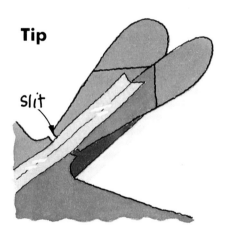

Slit

If you put the tape on carefully, it will hold the wings and tail at the right dihedral angle. It will also keep the tail pointing up slightly at the slit.

Elevators

when it flies correctly, tape over the nose.

5. Bend the ends of the tail up slightly along the remaining score lines to make elevators.

6. Put plasticine inside the nose to add weight. Then test fly it. If it dives, bend the elevators up more. If it stalls, take some plasticine away.

Tiny trainers

These two tiny planes are made from a single piece of paper and are quick to put together. Use normal paper, such as ordinary writing paper or photocopy paper for both of them.

V jet

Cut here

1. Copy the pink template on page 29, onto a piece of folded paper. Place the bottom edge of the template on the fold.

2. Score along the blue lines and cut along the red slit. The bottom blue line changes angle at the slit, so score each side separately.

3. Bend the wings and tail out to the sides along the score lines. The wings should point up slightly. The tail should make a 'V'.

V-shaped tail

Wing

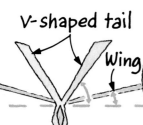

Tape holds the wings and tail at the right angle.

Add plasticine

4. Check that your plane looks like the picture above, from behind. Then use tape to hold the wings and tail at the correct angles.

5. Put plasticine inside the nose. Then test fly the plane. If it stalls, add more plasticine; if it dives, take some away.

6. When the V jet is properly balanced, you can try steering it with the tail. It tells you how on the right.

Steering V jet

Twist one side of the tail up and the other side down to make the V jet turn.

Curl the tip of the tail between your finger and thumb like this:

Tail

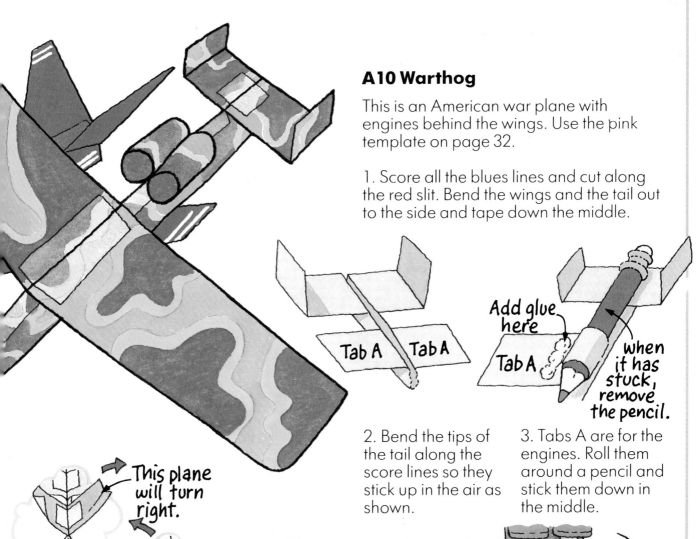

A10 Warthog

This is an American war plane with engines behind the wings. Use the pink template on page 32.

1. Score all the blues lines and cut along the red slit. Bend the wings and the tail out to the side and tape down the middle.

Tab A   Tab A

Add glue here

Tab A

when it has stuck, remove the pencil.

2. Bend the tips of the tail along the score lines so they stick up in the air as shown.

3. Tabs A are for the engines. Roll them around a pencil and stick them down in the middle.

This plane will turn right.

This plane will turn left.

Bend both sides up to make it climb or down to make it dive.

Launch tips

Light planes like these fly best if not thrown hard. Hold them underneath the wings. Move your whole arm forwards when you launch them and then just let go.

The higher you launch it, the further it will fly. Try standing on a chair and see how far it will glide.

11

Camber jet

This plane has a curved wing, called a cambered wing, which makes it fly better. See below if you want to know why.

What makes a wing lift

When the wing goes forward, some air goes over the top of it and some goes below it.

This air is thinner. It pulls the wing up. →

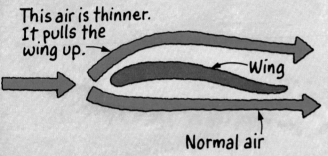

Wing

Normal air

If the wing is curved, the air on the top has further to go than the air below. So the top air stretches out to catch up with the bottom air. This makes it thinner, like a vaccuum, and sucks the wing up.

Weighted nose

Tailplane

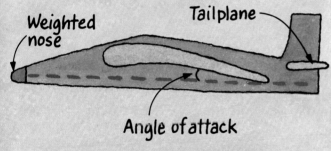

Angle of attack

The tailplane, or elevators, and the heavy nose balance the wing so that it stays at the angle that will give it the best lift. This is called 'the angle of attack'.

1. Copy the purple template on page 30 onto stiff paper. Only trace the solid lines, the dotted ones are for the next model.

2. Cut along the red lines. Score the blues ones very firmly so that it makes a crease on both sides of the fold.

Pre-flight check

Look under the wings of your plane for the dots you traced from the template. These mark the centre of balance. Place the wings on the tips of two pencils, alongside the dots.

Dot from template

Make sure the pencils are the same length.

Stick the pencils in plasticine.

If the plane falls backwards, add plasticine to the nose. If it falls forwards take some away. When it balances, the wings will be at the right angle of attack.

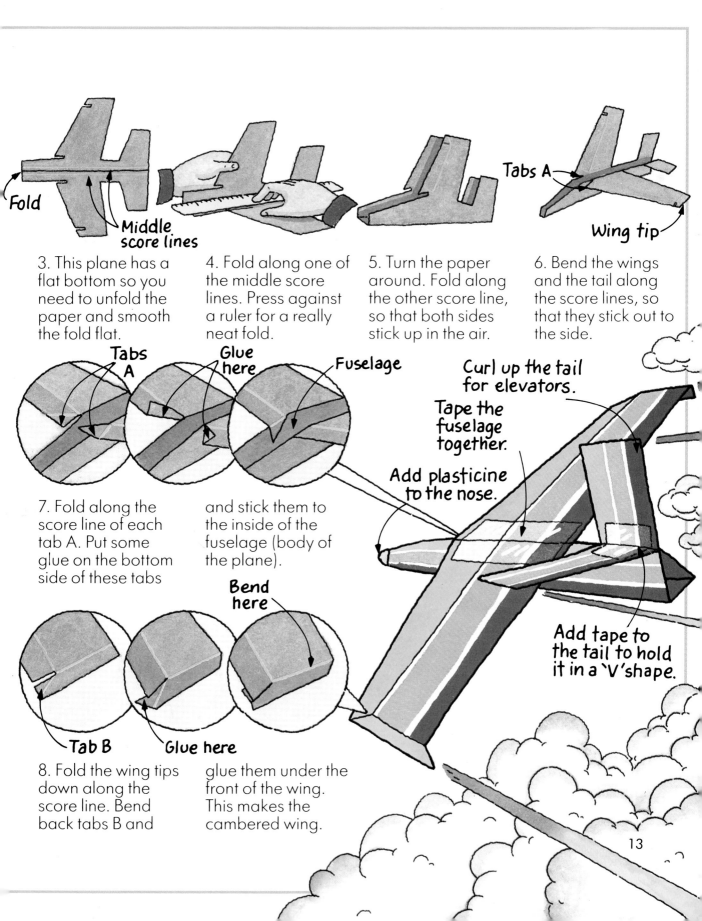

Fold

Middle score lines

Tabs A

Wing tip

3. This plane has a flat bottom so you need to unfold the paper and smooth the fold flat.

4. Fold along one of the middle score lines. Press against a ruler for a really neat fold.

5. Turn the paper around. Fold along the other score line, so that both sides stick up in the air.

6. Bend the wings and the tail along the score lines, so that they stick out to the side.

Tabs A

Glue here

Fuselage

Curl up the tail for elevators.

Tape the fuselage together.

Add plasticine to the nose.

7. Fold along the score line of each tab A. Put some glue on the bottom side of these tabs

and stick them to the inside of the fuselage (body of the plane).

Bend here

Add tape to the tail to hold it in a 'V' shape.

Tab B

Glue here

8. Fold the wing tips down along the score line. Bend back tabs B and

glue them under the front of the wing. This makes the cambered wing.

13

Stunt bug

This plane has extra features which make it fly all sorts of stunts. You need to make it from thin cardboard because it has to fly hard and fast.

Elevators

Bend here for the 'T' tail.

Rudder
Bend the rudder here.

1. Start by copying the purple template on page 30 which you used for the camber jet, but this time trace, score and cut all the dotted lines too.

2. Make it like the camber jet, except for the tail. Fold that out to the side along the dotted blue score line to make a T-shape.

3. The bits at the back of the tail are for the rudder. Stick them together. The score lines on the top of the 'T' are for the elevators.

Stunts to do

Before you try these stunts make sure your plane is well balanced and can fly in a straight line. Then try bending the elevators, ailerons or rudder as described on the right.

For all of the stunts you need to launch the plane hard and fast and you need lots of space. A big empty room is best, but you could fly it outside on a calm, dry day.

Loop the loop
Have both elevators up. Hold beneath the wings and launch level.

Snap loop
Have both elevators up and both ailerons down. Launch level.

***The Immelman**
Have both elevators up and one aileron down. Launch level.

Barrel roll
Have the elevators up and the rudder to one side. Launch with the nose pointing up slightly.

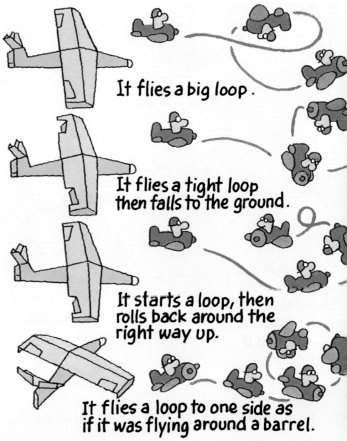

It flies a big loop.

It flies a tight loop then falls to the ground.

It starts a loop, then rolls back around the right way up.

It flies a loop to one side as if it was flying around a barrel.

14

* This one is named after the German pilot who invented it.

Bend up or down here.

Aileron

4. The ailerons are the little flaps on the wings. You bend them up or down along the dotted blue line.

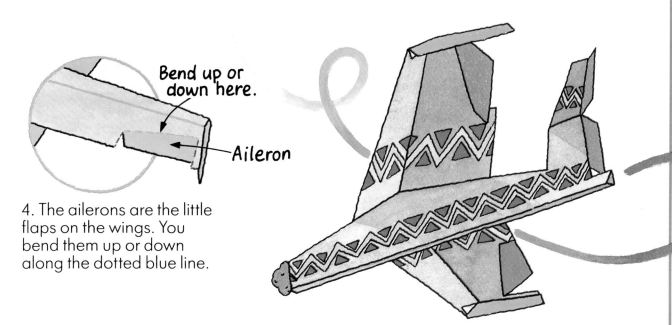

Slow roll
Have one aileron up, and one down. Launch slightly upwards.

The 'S' bend
Have the rudder to the left. Launch it with the right wing towards the ground.

The 'G' turn
Have the elevators up. Launch with one wing tip pointing straight to the floor.

The outside loop
Have the elevators down; ailerons up. Hold the nose, and launch it straight up.

It flies forwards, rolling sideways as it goes.

It flies to the right and then to the left.

It flies a circle in front of you and comes back to the same place.

It flies a loop with the wings on the outside.

Other ideas
You could set up an obstacle course and see how many launches it takes to get around it. Here are some obstacles you could try.

Fly an 'S' bend around two chairs.

Fly a left or right turn through the door.

Fly a loop around the washing line.

Seagull

You need the orange template on page 31 and thick paper, folded in half. A large envelope is ideal as long as you keep away from any overlapping edges.

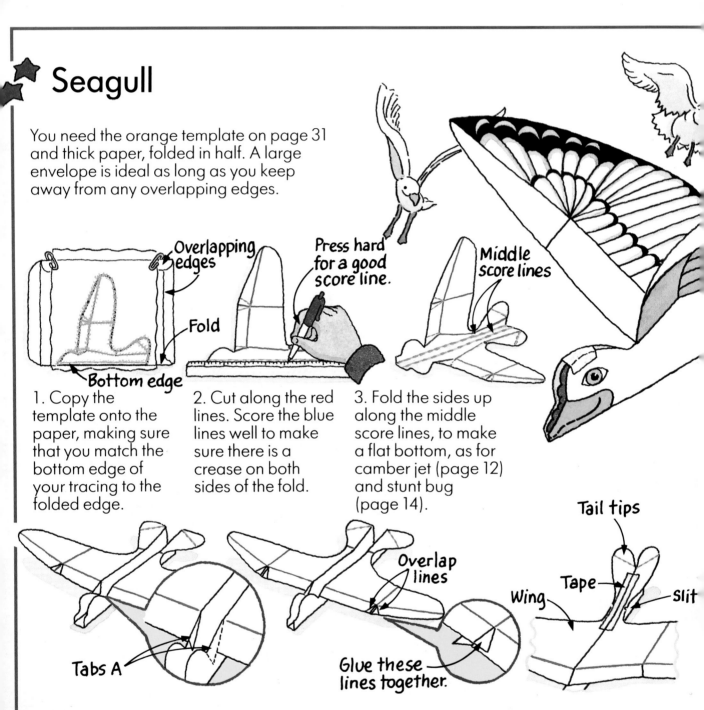

1. Copy the template onto the paper, making sure that you match the bottom edge of your tracing to the folded edge.

2. Cut along the red lines. Score the blue lines well to make sure there is a crease on both sides of the fold.

3. Fold the sides up along the middle score lines, to make a flat bottom, as for camber jet (page 12) and stunt bug (page 14).

4. Bend the wings and tail out to the side. Then glue tabs A inside the body, as you did for the camber jet.

5. Find the two overlap lines either side of the slit, in the middle of the wing. Put some glue on one and slide the

other over until the two lines meet. Hold them together until stuck. This gives the wings their bent shape.

6. Bend the tips of the tail up. Tape over the slit where the tail and wings join, to make the tail stick up slightly.

16

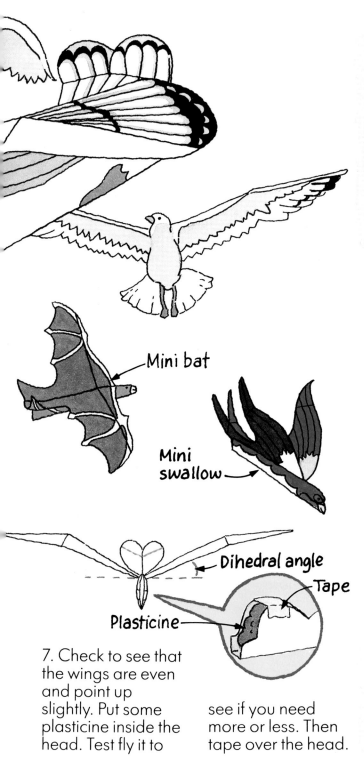

Other ideas

You could use different shapes for other birds. Try making up the mini templates below.

Small ones are harder to fly so be very neat and careful when you make them. Remember to add plasticine to the head. You could colour in the feathers with felt tip pens.

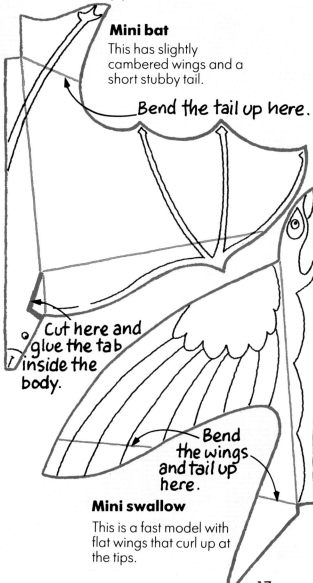

Mini bat
This has slightly cambered wings and a short stubby tail.

Bend the tail up here.

Cut here and glue the tab inside the body.

Bend the wings and tail up here.

Mini swallow
This is a fast model with flat wings that curl up at the tips.

Mini bat

Mini swallow

Dihedral angle

Tape

Plasticine

7. Check to see that the wings are even and point up slightly. Put some plasticine inside the head. Test fly it to see if you need more or less. Then tape over the head.

17

Concorde

Concorde is the world's fastest passenger plane. It flies from London to New York in 3 hours, 50 minutes. This model won't go that far but it is pretty fast. You need to glue it very carefully to make the wings the right shape.

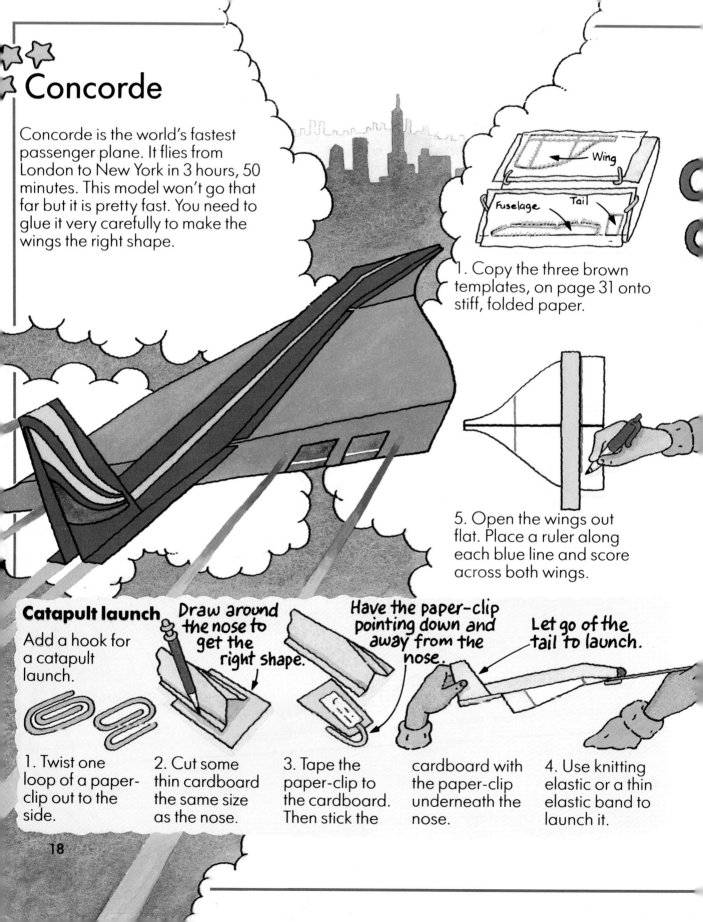

1. Copy the three brown templates, on page 31 onto stiff, folded paper.

5. Open the wings out flat. Place a ruler along each blue line and score across both wings.

Catapult launch

Add a hook for a catapult launch.

Draw around the nose to get the right shape.

Have the paper-clip pointing down and away from the nose.

Let go of the tail to launch.

1. Twist one loop of a paper-clip out to the side.

2. Cut some thin cardboard the same size as the nose.

3. Tape the paper-clip to the cardboard. Then stick the cardboard with the paper-clip underneath the nose.

4. Use knitting elastic or a thin elastic band to launch it.

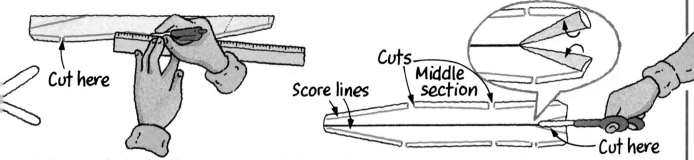

Cut here

Cuts — Middle section

Score lines

Cut here

2. Start with the fuselage. Score each blue line separately. Cut along the red ones.

3. Fold the edges out along the score lines. Do this bit by bit, starting with the section in the middle between the cuts.

4. Cut along the nose end of the fold, to where the blue lines meet the fold. Bend the corners in along the blue lines and glue them inside.

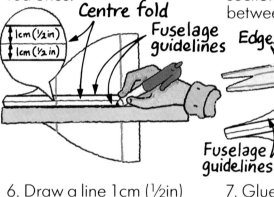

Centre fold

Fuselage guidelines

1cm (½in)
1cm (½in)

Edges

Fuselage guidelines

It bends up at the back.

It bends down at the front.

6. Draw a line 1cm (½in) away from the centre fold, on each side. These are the guidelines for the fuselage.

7. Glue the fuselage to the wings. Make sure that each edge meets the guideline you drew earlier. See the tip

below for help. The shape of the fuselage makes the wings bend down at the nose and up at the tail end.

Glue the tail on here.

Add plasticine

8. Finally, take the tail fin. Put glue inside and stick it to the end of the fuselage, behind the wings. Have the

sloping edge towards the nose. Put plasticine in the nose and test fly it.

Tip

To match each edge with the guidelines stick one section at a time, starting in the middle. Hold it together with your thumb and fingers until it has stuck.

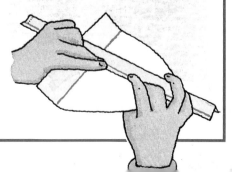

Sky rocket

This is a fast and furious model that you can fly outdoors. Make sure that you fold and glue it neatly, because even a small mistake will change the way it flies.

1. Copy the yellow template on page 31 onto thin cardboard, folded in half. Score all the blue lines carefully.

Use the edge of a table for a straight fold.

Diamond-shaped tube

2. Fold along the long blue lines to make a diamond-shaped tube for the fuselage.

Tail

Wings

Fuselage

3. Fold the wings and the tail out to the sides along the score lines.

Add tape

Hook

4. Bend one side of a paper-clip out to make a hook. Tape around the rest of the paper-clip.

Leave the end of the nose open.

Pinch the edges together until they stick.

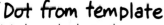

Dot from template

5. Make a hole in the fuselage, at the dot you traced from the template. Push the hook through it.

Have the hook pointing this way.

Make sure it is pointing away from the nose, then stick the taped side of the paper-clip inside.

Glue the tail fin together too.

6. Glue the top of the fuselage and the tail fin together. Leave the nose open for plasticine.

20

Smooth plasticine around the nose for a soft, safe point.

7. Put the plane upside down on thin cardboard and draw around the edge of the wings. Cut out the shape you have drawn and stick it on top of the wings. Then do exactly the same for the tail.

8. Put plasticine in the nose and test fly the plane. Adjust the amount until it flies well. Then tape around the nose.

Launch it at the top of a slope for an even longer glide.

If there is a gentle breeze, have the nose pointing into the wind.

Super launcher

This is a long-distance launcher which you can try outside on a calm, dry day.

You need a 50cm (1½ft) stick or post, 9m (27ft) of strong thread and 3m (9ft) of 3mm (⅛ in) -wide elastic. You can buy this in model plane shops or ask a sewing shop for thin elastic.

Post

Elastic

Too fast a launch may crash the plane, so pull back gently at first.

Metal paper-clip

Strong thread

Tie the thread to the elastic, which you then tie to the top of the post. Add a metal paper-clip to the other end of the thread.

Stick the post firmly into the ground and put the paper-clip onto the launch hook of your plane.

Pull the plane away from the post until the elastic is stretched. Point the nose up slightly and let go to launch.

21

Swing wing

This model is the same as the sky rocket, only you add wings which move. You need to make the sky rocket on page 20 first. Then add two wings. Follow the steps below for each wing.

To make each wing

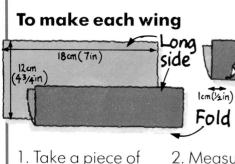

Long side

18cm (7in)

12cm (4¾in)

Open edge

1cm (½in)

1cm (½in)

Fold

Folded edge

1. Take a piece of stiff paper, 18 x 12cm (7 x 4¾ in). Fold it in half, with the longest sides together.

2. Measure 1cm (½in) from the left corner of the folded edge and from the right corner of the open edge.

3. Draw a line from each measurement to the opposite corner as shown above. Then cut along the lines.

To fix the wings to the sky rocket

Use a pin or cocktail stick to make the hole.

Dots from template

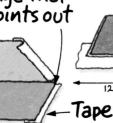

Edge that points out

Tape

12cm (4¾ in)

Open corner

1cm (½in)

1cm (½in)

4. Open the paper out. Put some tape over the edge that points outwards.

5. Fold the paper in half again. Cut some tape 12cm (4¾ in) long. Use it to stick the long edges together, starting at the corner without tape.

6. Find the open corner. Measure 1cm (½in) in from each edge. Make a hole where the two measures meet, using a pin or cocktail stick.

1. Make a hole in the rocket wings at the dots you copied from the template.

At the top of its launch, swing wing slows up, the wings swing out and it glides to the ground.

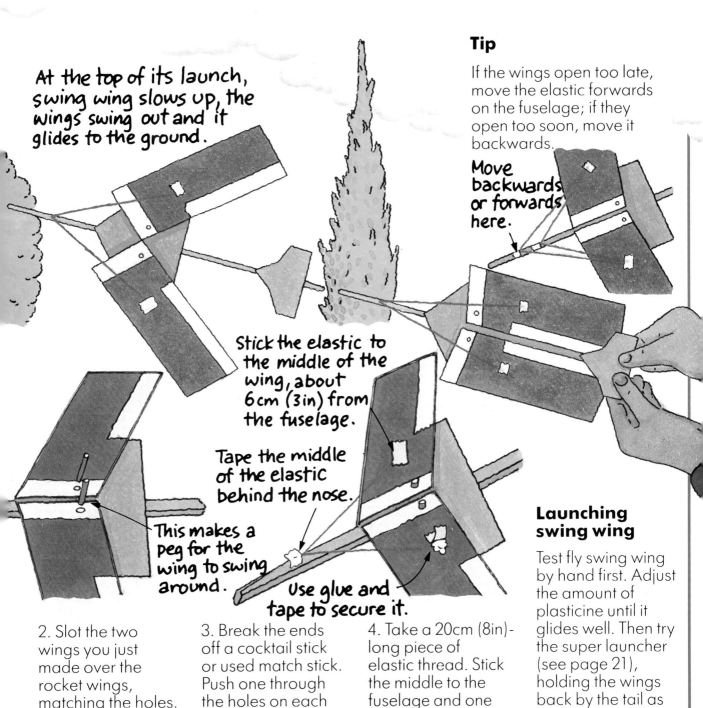

Tip

If the wings open too late, move the elastic forwards on the fuselage; if they open too soon, move it backwards.

Move backwards or forwards here.

Stick the elastic to the middle of the wing, about 6cm (3in) from the fuselage.

Tape the middle of the elastic behind the nose.

This makes a peg for the wing to swing around.

Use glue and tape to secure it.

Launching swing wing

Test fly swing wing by hand first. Adjust the amount of plasticine until it glides well. Then try the super launcher (see page 21), holding the wings back by the tail as you launch it.

2. Slot the two wings you just made over the rocket wings, matching the holes.

3. Break the ends off a cocktail stick or used match stick. Push one through the holes on each wing.

4. Take a 20cm (8in)-long piece of elastic thread. Stick the middle to the fuselage and one end to each wing.

Superglider

This model is quite difficult to make – there are 23 steps to follow – but it is three times bigger than anything else in this book. A well-made model can fly 100m (300ft). Only try making it when you can fold and glue neatly.

You need a large hall to fly it indoors. Or you could try flying it outside on a very calm day when the grass is dry. To start with, you need thin cardboard, thick paper, thin paper, a drinking straw, strong glue and the grey templates on page 32.

To make the wings

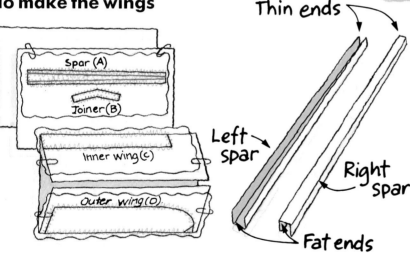

Tip

1. Copy templates A and B onto thin cardboard and C and D onto thick paper. Remember to copy each one twice – once for each wing.

2. Score the blue lines of each spar, A, firmly. Fold the edges up along the score lines on one spar, and down the other way on the other, to make a right and left spar.

Use a book to make a neat fold. Place it on one side of the score line. Use a ruler to fold up the other side. Press against the book edge.

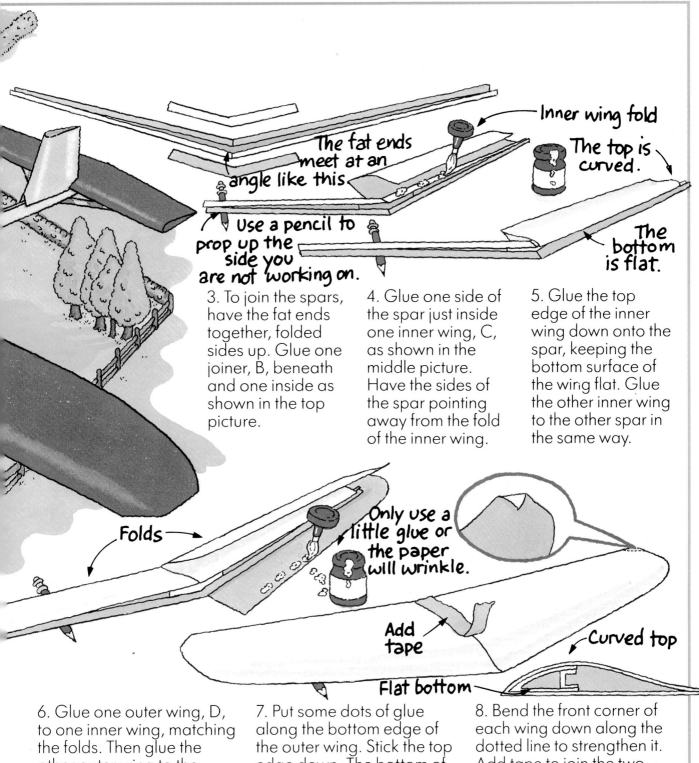

The fat ends meet at an angle like this.

Inner wing fold

The top is curved.

Use a pencil to prop up the side you are not working on.

The bottom is flat.

3. To join the spars, have the fat ends together, folded sides up. Glue one joiner, B, beneath and one inside as shown in the top picture.

4. Glue one side of the spar just inside one inner wing, C, as shown in the middle picture. Have the sides of the spar pointing away from the fold of the inner wing.

5. Glue the top edge of the inner wing down onto the spar, keeping the bottom surface of the wing flat. Glue the other inner wing to the other spar in the same way.

Folds

Only use a little glue or the paper will wrinkle.

Add tape

Curved top

Flat bottom

6. Glue one outer wing, D, to one inner wing, matching the folds. Then glue the other outer wing to the other side in the same way.

7. Put some dots of glue along the bottom edge of the outer wing. Stick the top edge down. The bottom of the wing should be flat; the top curved.

8. Bend the front corner of each wing down along the dotted line to strengthen it. Add tape to join the two wings in the middle.

25

To make the tail and tail fin

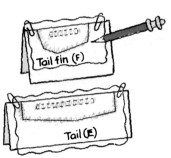

Guidelines

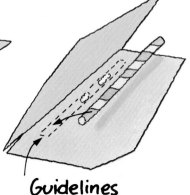

Guidelines

9. Copy templates E and F (the white templates shown inside template D) onto normal folded paper.

10. Trim the drinking straw to 17cm (6½in). Stick it inside the tail, E, along the guidelines marked.

11. Put some glue on the bottom edge of the tail. Stick the top edge down, keeping the bottom edge flat as you did for the wings.

12. Use a 4.5cm (2¾in) straw for the tail fin, F. Glue it inside, along the guidelines, as you did for the tail.

To make the fuselage

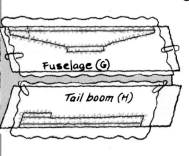

Tabs

Diamond-shaped tube

Tabs

14. Copy templates G and H onto thin cardboard. Score the blue lines firmly on both pieces.

15. Fold the sides up along the score lines on both pieces using a book and ruler (see the tip on page 24). It should make a diamond-shaped tube. Fold the tabs out on both pieces as shown.

16. Use a sharp pencil or pin to pierce a hole carefully in the fuselage, G, where it is marked X.

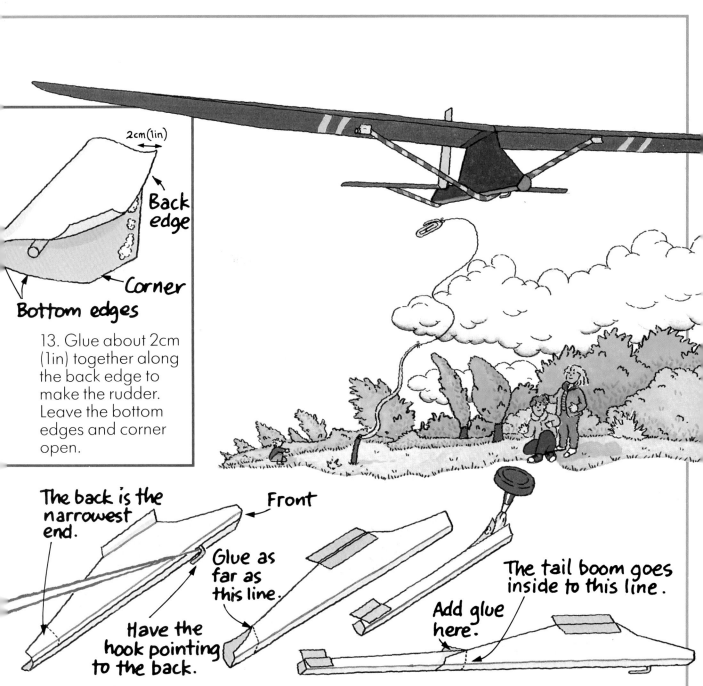

2cm(1in)

Back edge

Corner

Bottom edges

13. Glue about 2cm (1in) together along the back edge to make the rudder. Leave the bottom edges and corner open.

The back is the narrowest end.

Front

Glue as far as this line.

Have the hook pointing to the back.

The tail boom goes inside to this line.

Add glue here.

Bend a paper-clip into a hook, tape it and then stick it inside the fuselage as you did for the sky rocket on page 20.

17. Glue the top of the fuselage, G, together as far as the dotted line. Glue the top of the tail boom, H, together too.

18. Glue the tail boom, H inside the fuselage, G. The end of H should meet the line you glued up to on G, in the last step.

Now you have the finished fuselage, wings and tail. It tells you how to join them all on the next page.

To finish Superglider

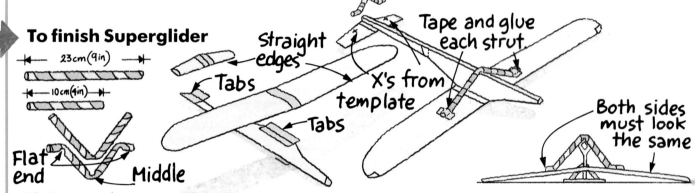

23cm (9in)

10cm (4in)

Flat end   Middle

Straight edges

Tabs

Tape and glue each strut

X's from template

Tabs

Both sides must look the same

19. You need two straws: one 23cm (9in) long; the other 10cm (4in). Bend both in half to find the middle. Bend back and flatten a small bit at each end.

20. Glue the wings and tail onto the tabs at the front and back of the fuselage. Have the straight edges of the tail and wings facing forwards.

21. Put glue on the middle and ends of the long straw. Turn the plane over carefully. Check that the wings are level, then stick the middle of the straw

to the fuselage and the ends to the crosses on each wing. Add tape. Glue and tape the short straw to the tail in the same way.

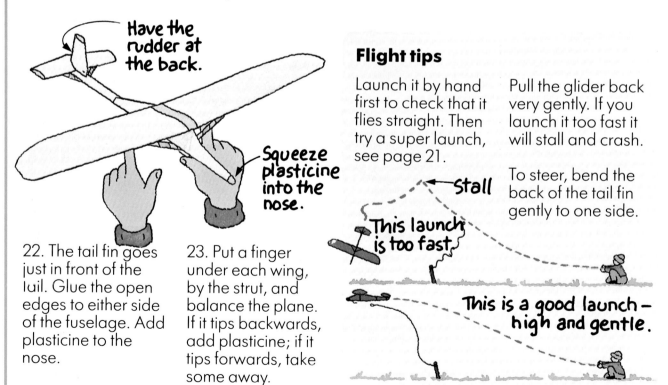

Have the rudder at the back.

Squeeze plasticine into the nose.

22. The tail fin goes just in front of the tail. Glue the open edges to either side of the fuselage. Add plasticine to the nose.

23. Put a finger under each wing, by the strut, and balance the plane. If it tips backwards, add plasticine; if it tips forwards, take some away.

Flight tips

Launch it by hand first to check that it flies straight. Then try a super launch, see page 21.

Pull the glider back very gently. If you launch it too fast it will stall and crash.

To steer, bend the back of the tail fin gently to one side.

Stall

This launch is too fast.

This is a good launch – high and gentle.

Templates

For lots of the models in this book, you need to trace the templates (outline shapes) on the next five pages.

How to trace a template

Keep the paper in place with paper-clips.

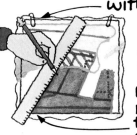

Use a ruler to trace straight lines.

1. Lay a piece of tracing paper over the template you want to use. Trace the outline with a pencil.

2. Turn the tracing over. Scribble over the outline with a soft pencil. Turn the tracing over again.

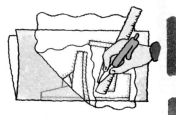

3. Lay the tracing over your paper. If there is an edge marked 'place on fold', use folded paper and place this edge on the fold.

4. Go over the traced lines again with a sharp pencil or ball point pen. Press hard so that a line appears on the paper beneath.

Notice that the blue line changes angle here.

V jet

Use normal paper.

Place on fold.

Tip

Lines shown in red are ones you have to cut along once you have copied the template.

Lines shown in blue are ones you have to score, once you have copied the template.

Thick lines show you which edge to put on the fold of your paper.

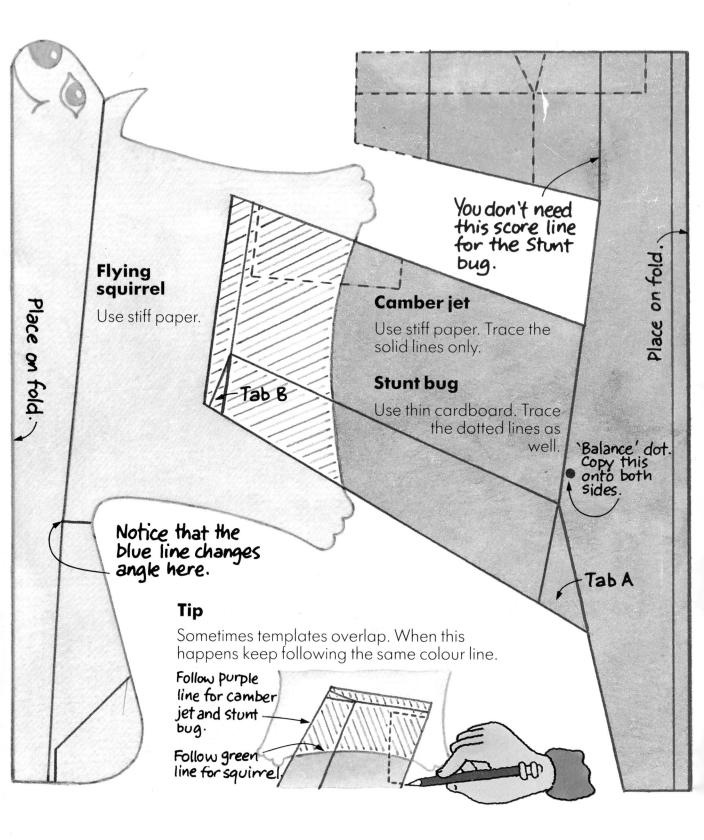

Flying squirrel

Use stiff paper.

Place on fold.

Notice that the blue line changes angle here.

Tab B

You don't need this score line for the Stunt bug.

Camber jet

Use stiff paper. Trace the solid lines only.

Stunt bug

Use thin cardboard. Trace the dotted lines as well.

'Balance' dot. Copy this onto both sides.

Place on fold.

Tab A

Tip

Sometimes templates overlap. When this happens keep following the same colour line.

Follow purple line for camber jet and stunt bug.

Follow green line for squirrel.

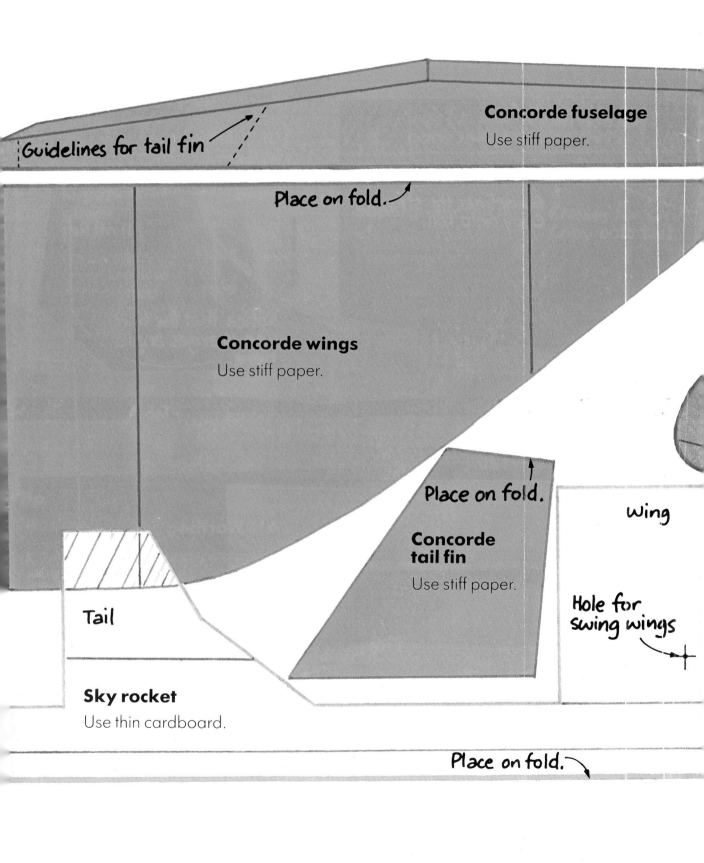

Guidelines for tail fin

Concorde fuselage
Use stiff paper.

Place on fold.

Concorde wings
Use stiff paper.

Place on fold.

Concorde tail fin
Use stiff paper.

Wing

Hole for swing wings

Tail

Sky rocket
Use thin cardboard.

Place on fold.

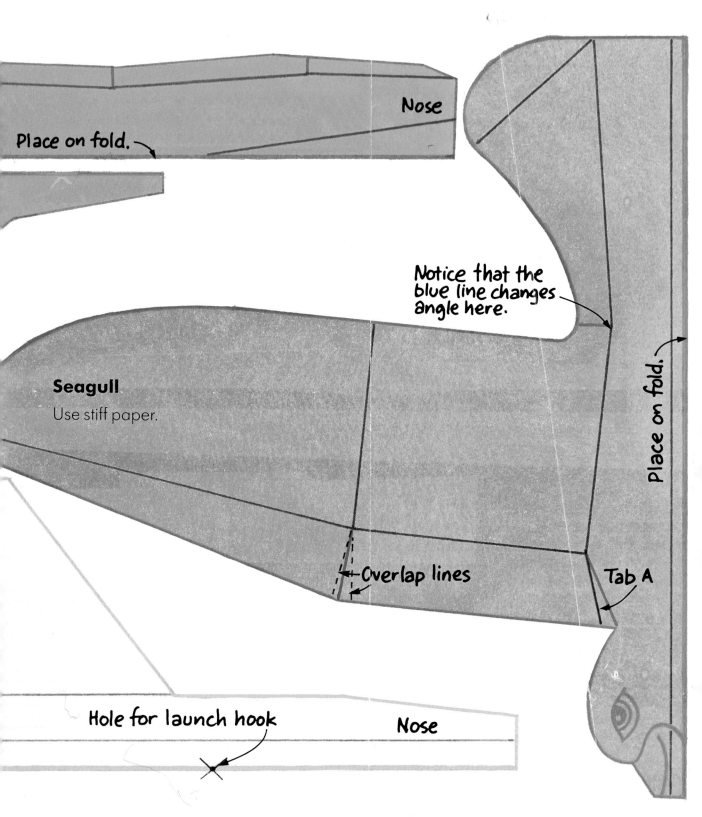

Nose

Place on fold.

Notice that the
blue line changes
angle here.

Seagull
Use stiff paper.

Place on fold.

Overlap lines

Tab A

Hole for launch hook

Nose